Blessings

Kym Byrd

The Amazon Endure typeface was designed by 2K/DENMARK in 2025.
Template id: ST-414D415A-25-A01
Printed in The United States.
ISBN: 979-89935732-0-5

DEDICATION

To Jesus for showing me that there is always glitter in all things lighting the way and making the most painful things sparkle with some beauty. Your love and kindness undoes me daily.

CONTENTS

ACKNOWLEDGMENTS

Thank you to Paul who told me I could write and believed in me for 31 years when I didn't believe in myself. You never give up on me. I love you for it!

To Journeymates and Pam who changed my life by teaching me to be still, listen and pay attention to what bubbles up. There are so many bubbles. And for giving me the place to read these surrounded only by love.

For all my dear friends who let me come out of hiding and are my biggest cheer leaders in life. You listened and held this tender place in me with love and care. You inspired me to be brave.
Marco Polo Girls, Pink Slipper Group & My Tuesday Sister Wife

HOW TO USE THIS BOOK

This book is interactive. It is something to approach slowly. There is no particular order. Some people flip through it and when a picture speaks to them they stop. Some people take one blessing at a time and think about it and see what it stirs in them. The book is a form of Visio Divina. This is a contemplative practice where you pray looking at a piece of art. I love this practice because it allows me to tap into my childlike imagination with God as well as it stirs my emotions more than just words. My hope is that you will find God in these blessings and make them your own.

For those of you that like a process here are some questions and ideas to try out.

Visio Divina Process:

1. **Pick a page you are drawn to today.**
2. **Ask God to interact with you as you read the blessings and look at the picture.**
3. **Interact with the Picture.** Take a long loving look at the picture. Are you drawn or repulsed by it? What do you notice? Does it stir any emotions in you? What does it feel like physically to you in your body? Does it remind you of anything in your current life?
4. **Take time to slowly read the words of the blessing.** What words or phrases stick out to you? Are there any words that you don't like? Are there any desires or longings that pop out to you that you want?
5. **Take time to journal what comes up for you. Blank pages included for you to write or doodle.**

Other Uses:

1. **Pray these over people you want to bless.** I originally wrote these to close a prayer group. I would have the ladies stand and I would read over them. I have also used it with spiritual direction clients as well. It's lovely to insert your name or someone's name in it to personalize it.
2. **Create your own blessings and pictures with God.** Everyone is creative in their own way. Ultimately you are just collaborating with God. He loves and knows you and is honored to create with you.

Pleasant words are a honeycomb, sweet to the soul and healing to the body.

Proverbs 16:24

Whoever brings blessing will be enriched, and one who waters will himself be watered.

Proverbs 11:25

and let's consider how to encourage one another in love and good deeds

Hebrews 10:24

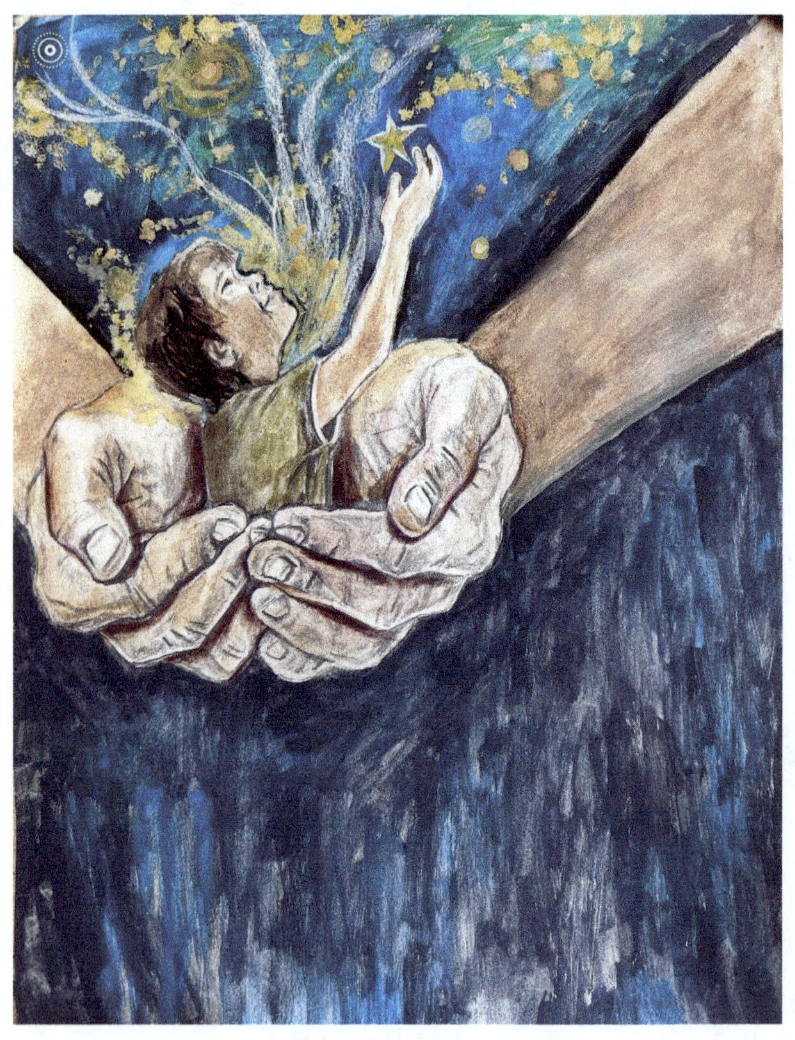

Hold These for Me

Hold my longings.
Hold my unanswered prayers.
The questions that linger.
The wounds and the joys.
Hold them close for me.
The pain, the disappointments and grief.
My anger, grievances and doubts.
My adventures and my well
thought out plans.
Protect them.
Guard them in the
treasure chest of Your heart.
Until next time when we can sift and
sort, mold and create them again together.
But mostly, just hold on to me.

Amen

Questions to Ponder

1. What are some of your longings?

2. What prayers are you waiting for changes to happen in that seem like nothing is happening?

3. What are some of your burning questions?

4. What are some of your joys and adventures?

5. What would it feel like to entrust God with these? What is hard about that?

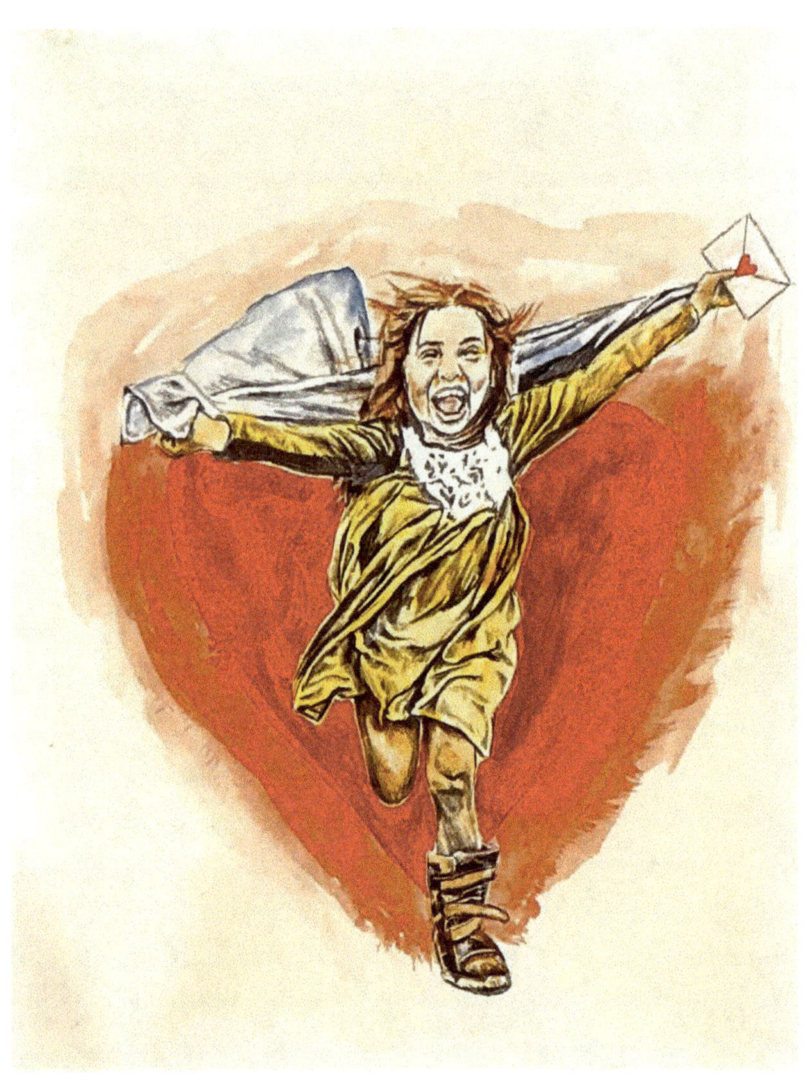

LOVE POEM

Love me carefully in my tender wounds
In my aging
In my nothing to offer-ness
In my creativity and my wonder
In my questioning and my blunder

Love Me. Love Me.

Love me when I cling to what is poor
When I scream and slam the door
When I walk away and hide

Love Me. Love Me. Love Me.

I am Your Bride,
xoxoxooxox

Questions to Ponder

~What areas of my life do I deem unlovable?

~What tender places in you need to be loved?

~What things would change in your body, soul and emotions if you were to allow yourself to be loved deeply by God? By others?

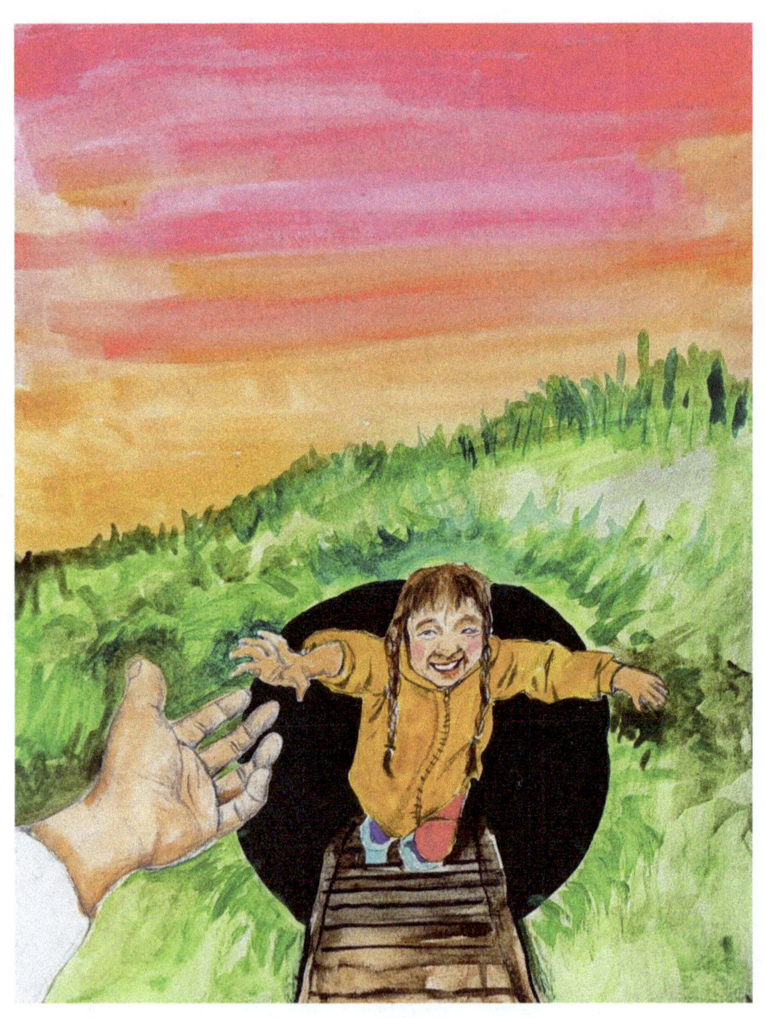

May Your Love

May Your love rescue me when I am in over my head.

May Your love lead me to wide open spaces so
I can breathe again.

May Your love comfort me and quiet me
When uncertainty crowds me in.

May Your love slow me down so I might be still and pay close attention.

May Your love call me back home when I am far away.

May Your love open my heart wide open to receive it.

Amen

Questions to sit a bit with

- **Where are you in need of rescue?**
- **Where are you running so fast that you need to slow down?**
- **What calls you back home to God?**

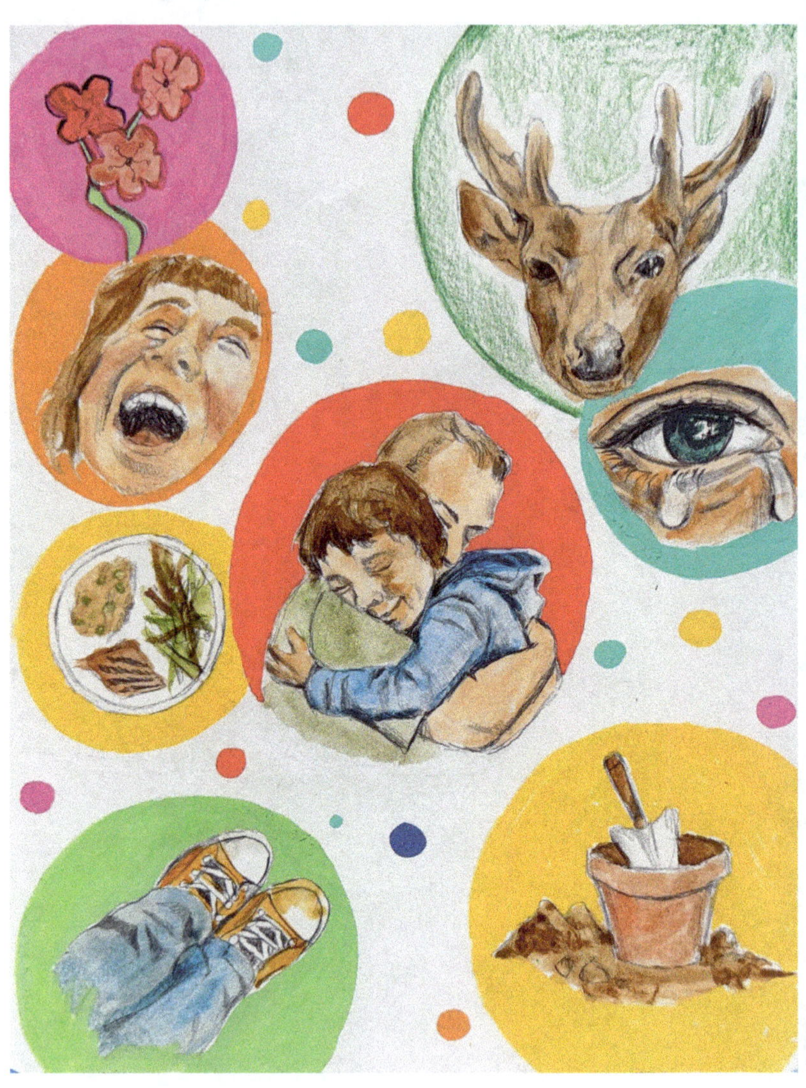

nowhere and everywhere

when I eat a home cooked meal,
there You are.

when I see the first blossoms of spring,
there You are.

when I feel most alone and weary,
there You are.

in a hug,
in a tear,
in chocolate,
in a deer,
there You are.

in my sorrow,
in my shame,
in my wants,
in my pain,
there You are.

in my laughter,
in my work,
in my shoes,
in the dirt,
there You are.

where can I go?
nowhere without You.
what can I do?
nothing without You.
I am yours and You are mine.

Grist for the Mill

1. Where do you see God in your life?

2. What areas in your life do you believe are off limits for God?

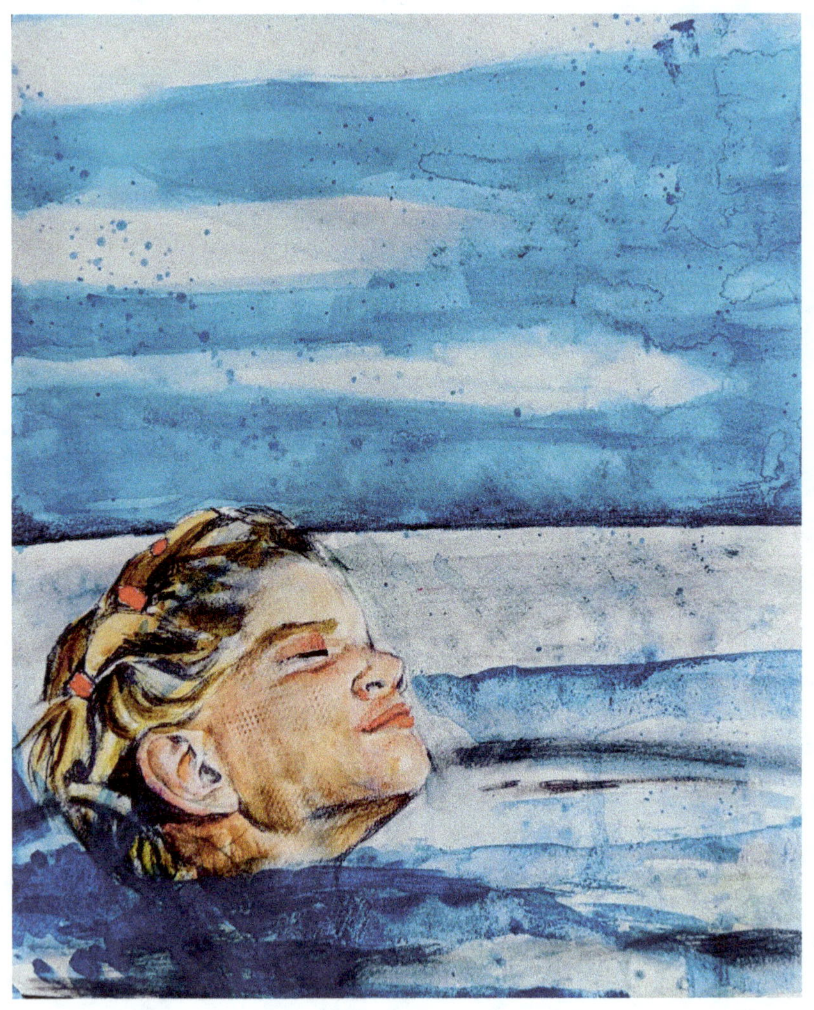

Breath

Slow me down. Give me deep breath to see, to hear and to know You.

Breathe in Your Presence.

Breathe out my tightly held agenda.

Breathe in Deep Rest.

Breathe out busyness and hustle.

Breathe in True Peace.

Breathe out the loud shouting that comes from the parts of me that are afraid.

Breathe in Goodness.

Breathe out my hoarding and scarcity.

Breathe in Your Kindness and Compassion.

Breathe out judgment and condemnation.

Breathe in Fresh Crisp Air.

Breathe out the staleness.

Slow me down long enough to see the path, to know the truth to set me free.

Breathe in You.

Give yourself some real time to Breathe.

Take 5 long deep breaths. Your belly should stick out like a happy toddler.

Notice places in your body that begin to still.

Where and when do you find yourself holding your breath?

What comes up for you?

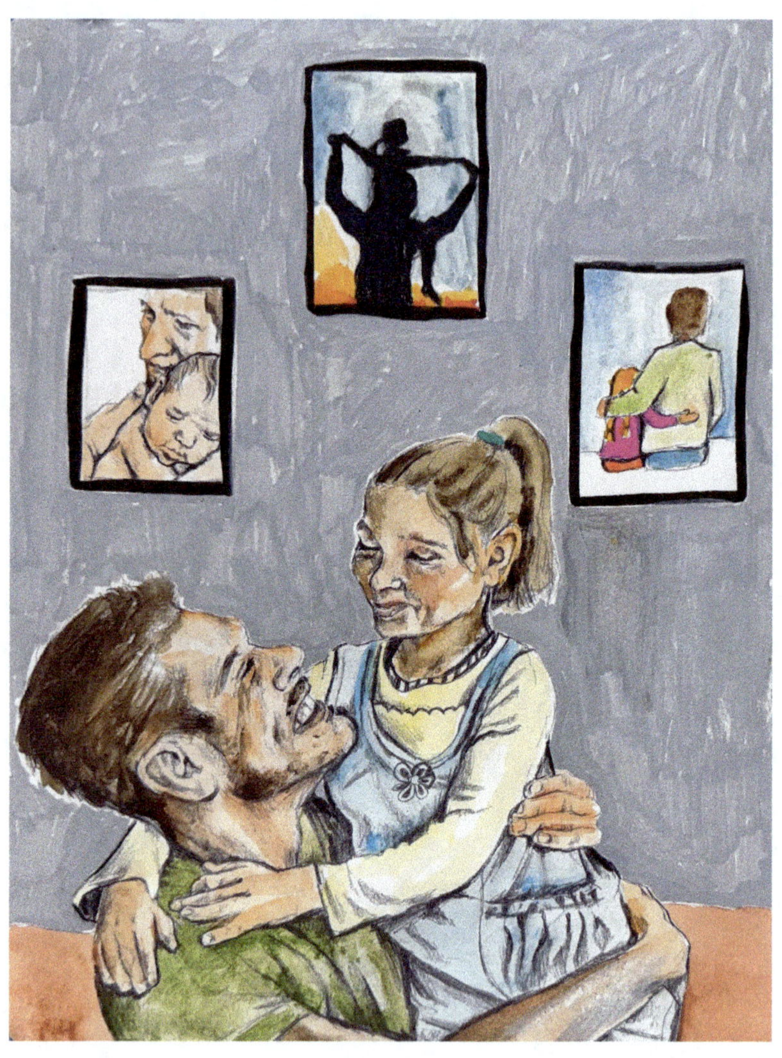

Reminders

Remind me again that I am free.

Remind me again that You are here with me
　　Undistracted
　　Un-imposed Upon
　　With a full gaze.

Remind me again that You delight in me.
　　I am not merely tolerated.

Remind me again that there is an abundance of Hope and Peace, mine for the taking,
　　Though the world would say otherwise.

Remind me again that EVERY single detail of my life is considered.
　　That my needs and longings are not extra.

Remind me again that I am deeply known in all of my Goodness
　　And all of my brokenness.

Remind me again and again that I am loved.

Amen

When you find yourself in harder times, what becomes forgetful to you?

What things do you do to keep the memory of holy experiences with God alive?

What do you need to be reminded of today?

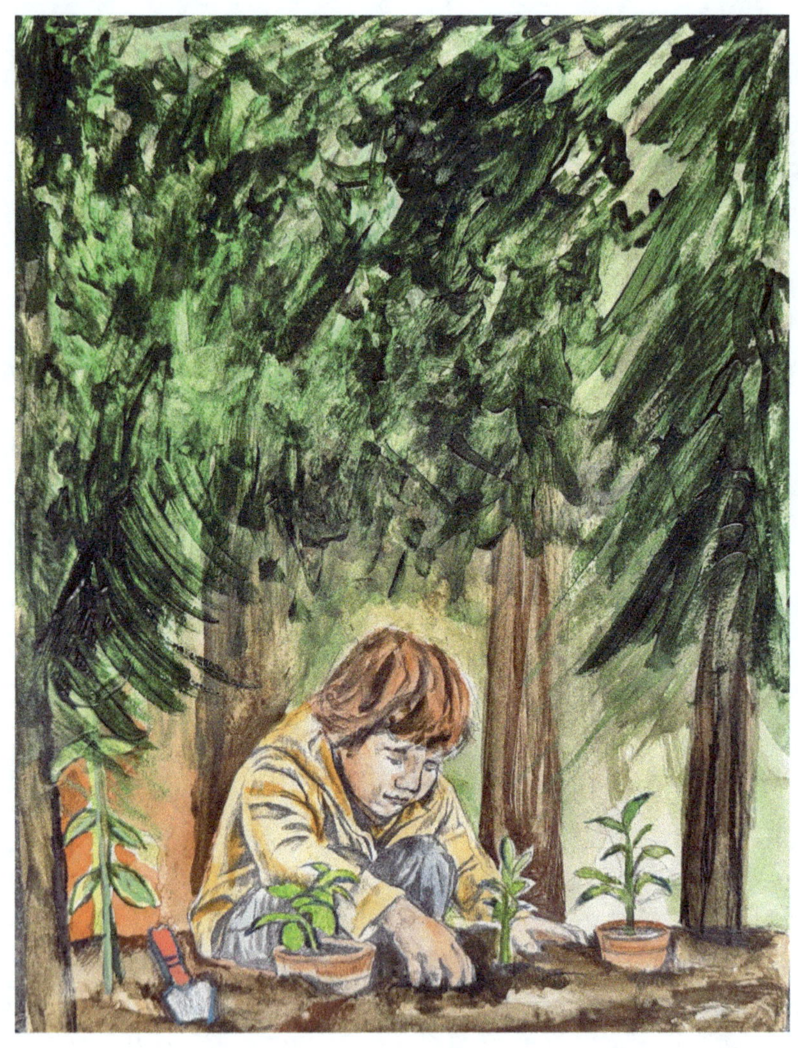

Unfinished Business

Bless you as you hold space for what is unknown.

Bless you as you trust God has a real plan.

Bless you as you surrender to "I don't know."

Bless you as you are just left with wonder.

Bless you as you leave it undone and unfinished.

Bless you as you stay or walk away.

May the unfinished, undone and unknown lead you back

To the One who knows, completes and loves you.

Amen.

What parts of life feel frustrating and undone?

What feelings and physical sensations arrive around what is undone?

What areas of surrender are invitations?

How can you show yourself kindness in the in-between places?

How is God showing up in this “with” you in your undone places?

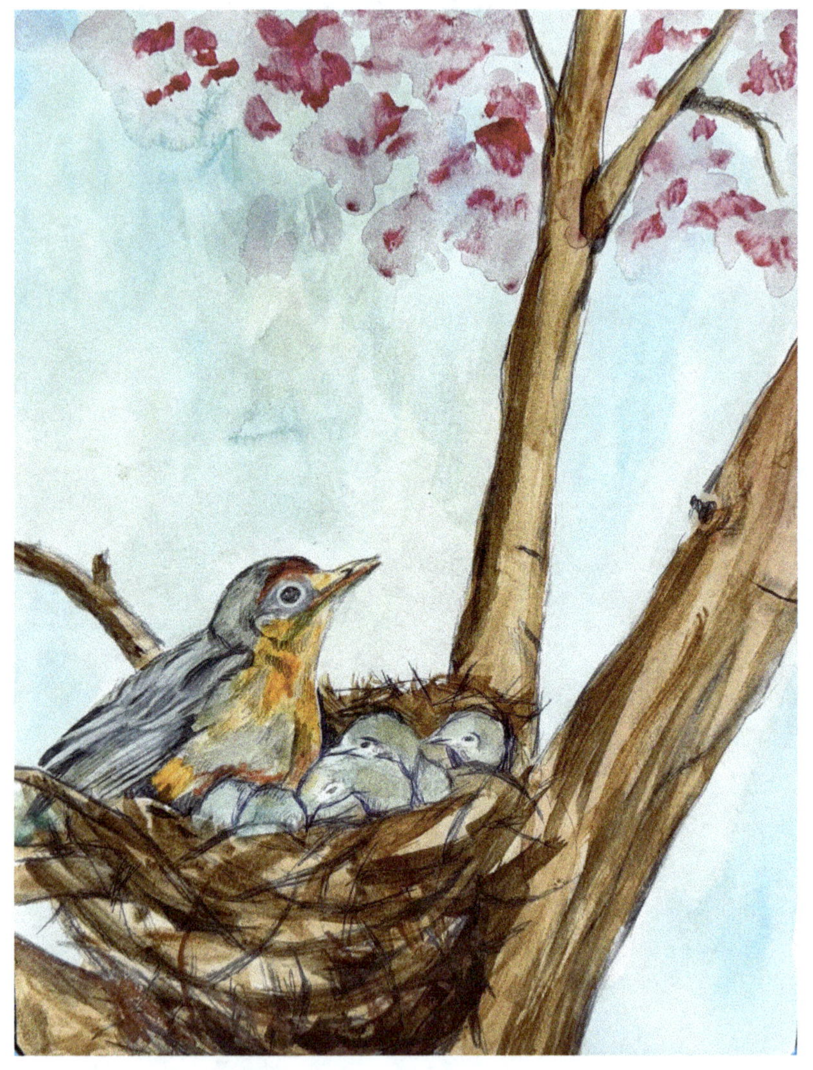

Close

Reader: In the ordinary, boring, “have to” mundane tasks
Group: You are closer to me than I am to myself.
Reader: In the loneliness of a crowded room
Group: You are closer to me than I am to myself.
Reader: When trouble, bad news and pain come a calling’
Group: You are closer to me than I am to myself.
Reader: When I blow it and the shame descends upon me
Group: You are closer to me than I am to myself.
Reader: In the baby birds and each blossoming flower
Group: You are closer to me than I am to myself.
Reader: When I have no idea, no next step, no where to go
Group: You are closer to me than I am to myself.
Reader: In the quiet when all those thoughts begin to swarm
Group: You are closer to me than I am to myself.
Reader: And when I finally sleep and rest from all of this day
Group: You are closer to me than I am to myself.

Amen.

“You are closer to me than I am to myself,” from St. Augustine’s Prayer

Where do you feel close to God?

Where do you feel distanced from Him?

What do things look like as you imagine Him closer than you are to yourself in these situations?

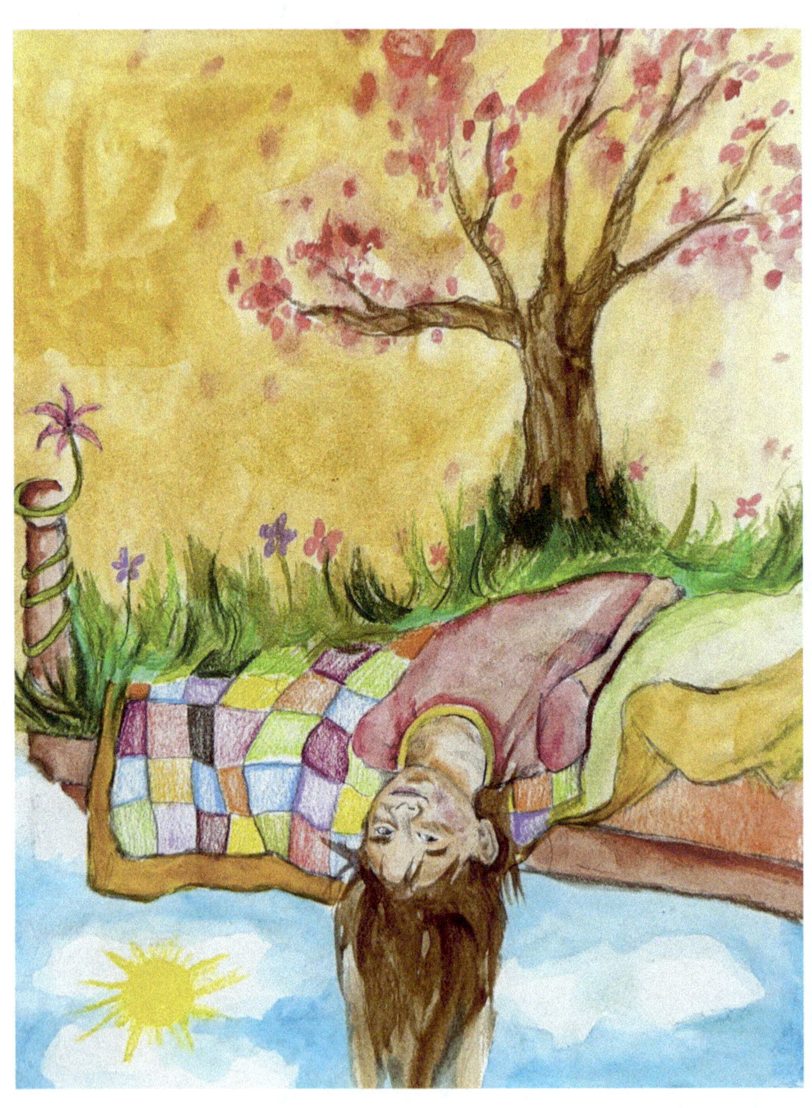

Upside Down

May I be ***OVERPROTECTIVE*** of
my time with You.
May I ***HOARD*** the graces You
place before me.
May I ***RUMINATE*** on how deeply I
am loved.
May ***ANXIETY*** remind me that I am
forgetting that You are with me.
May my ***CAPACITY INCREASE*** to
hold more of You.
More of Your love.
More of Your goodness.
More of Your kindness.
And May the ***EXCESS*** effortlessly
pour on those around me.

AMEN

What do the bold words mean to you? What do you associate them with?

What are some things that you can turn upside down for your good?

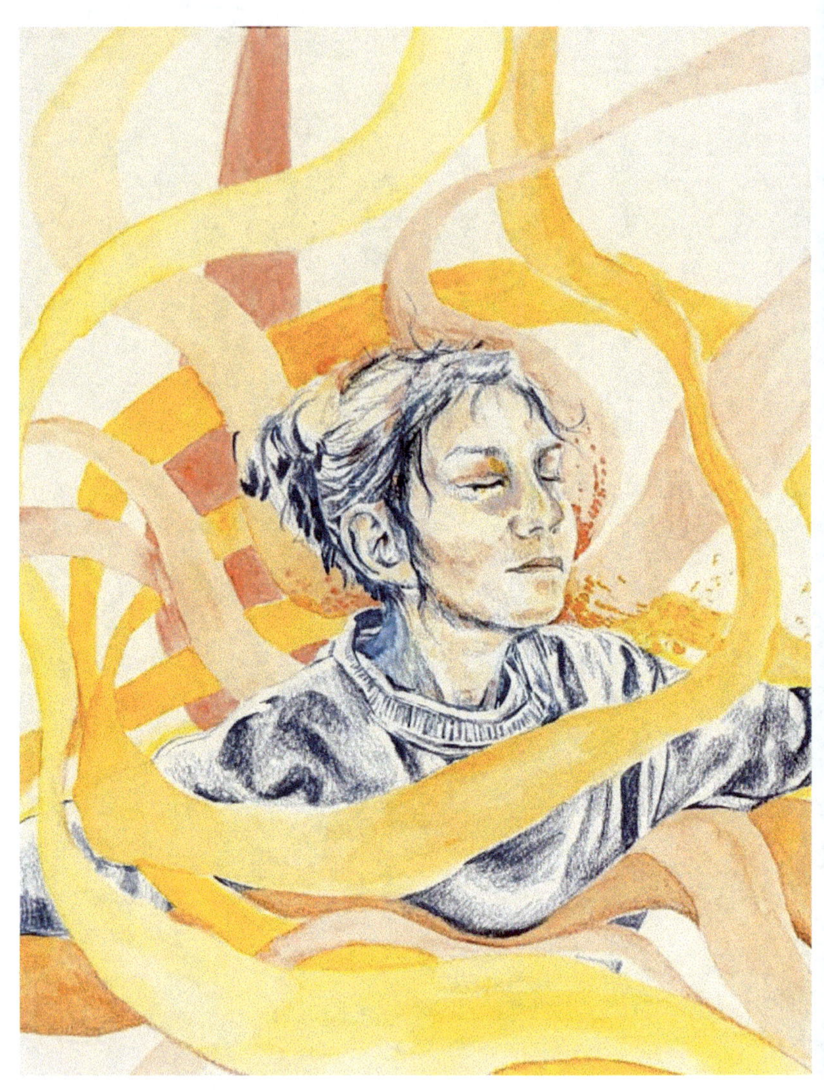

Capture Me

Round me up and bring me home

Take down the heart walls I have built to protect and control

Train my gaze upon the path of Your freedom, Your truth and Your love

Give me grace to accept Your kindness and affection

And the courage to stay just a bit longer

Amen

What places in you need to be captured?

When God captures you, how hard is it for you to stay with Him?

What do you run to to avoid it and why?

What does it feel like to be home with God?

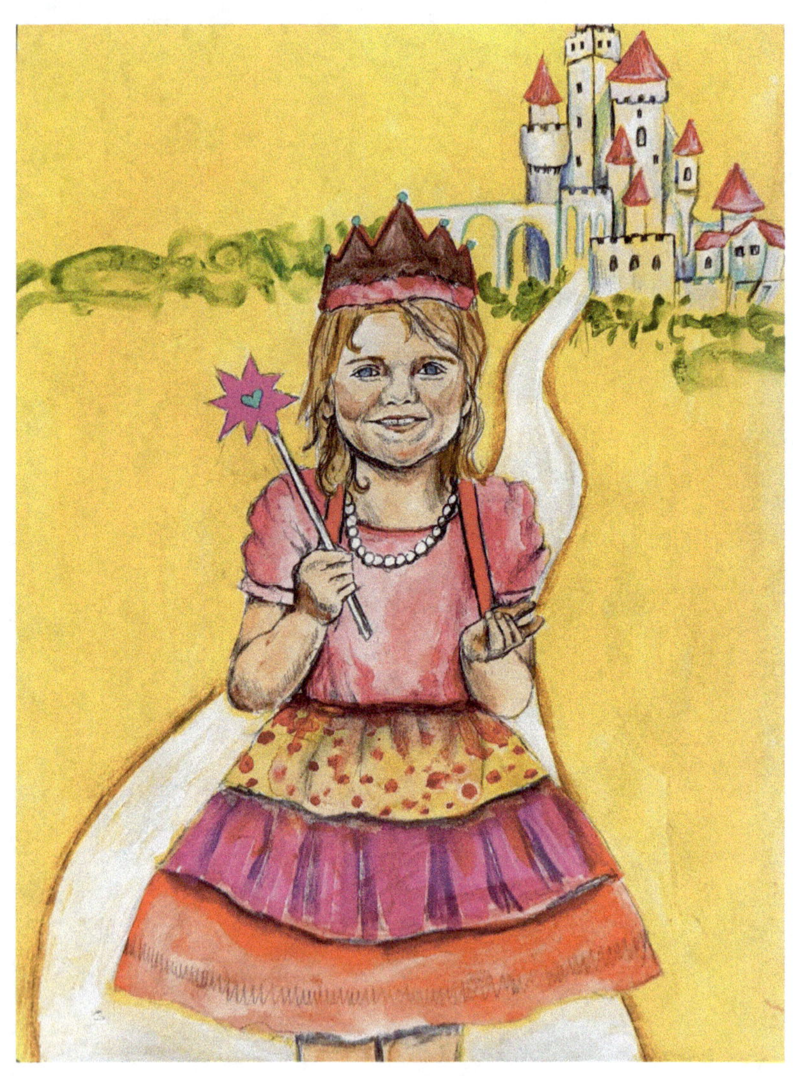

REALITY BLESSING

As I leave here today Lord help me to Remember.

May I remember I am a Daughter of a King.

May I remember my true self. I reflect You.

May I remember wherever I go You are with me
and I never walk alone.

You are with me guiding, loving and present to me.

May I remember You are always working in the
details of my life..

May I remember to be childlike, open, honest,
sincere and playful. For You choose to play with me.

May I remember how loved I am for You love me
more than I can contain or fathom.

Amen

How do you see yourself most days?

Ask God how He sees you.

Write down or doodle what He tells you.

What is the reality?

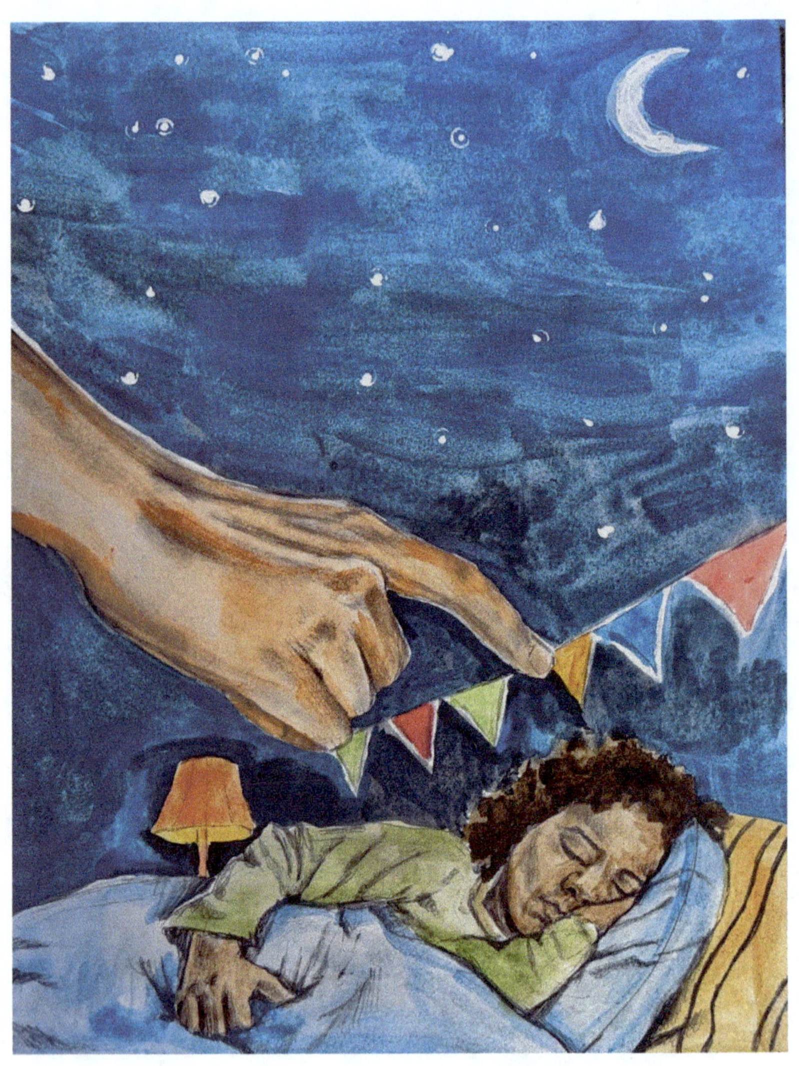

Wake Me Up

Wake Me Up.

Wake Me Up from my slumber.

Wake Me Up from my denial and
suppression.

Wake Me Up from my frozen state.

Wake Me Up to Feeling.

Wake Me up to Love.

Wake Me up to You.

How does God typically wake you up to show you something?

What are areas you avoid or find you try to repress?

How much pressure do you put on yourself to know things?

What practices help you open your eyes a bit more to cooperate with God?

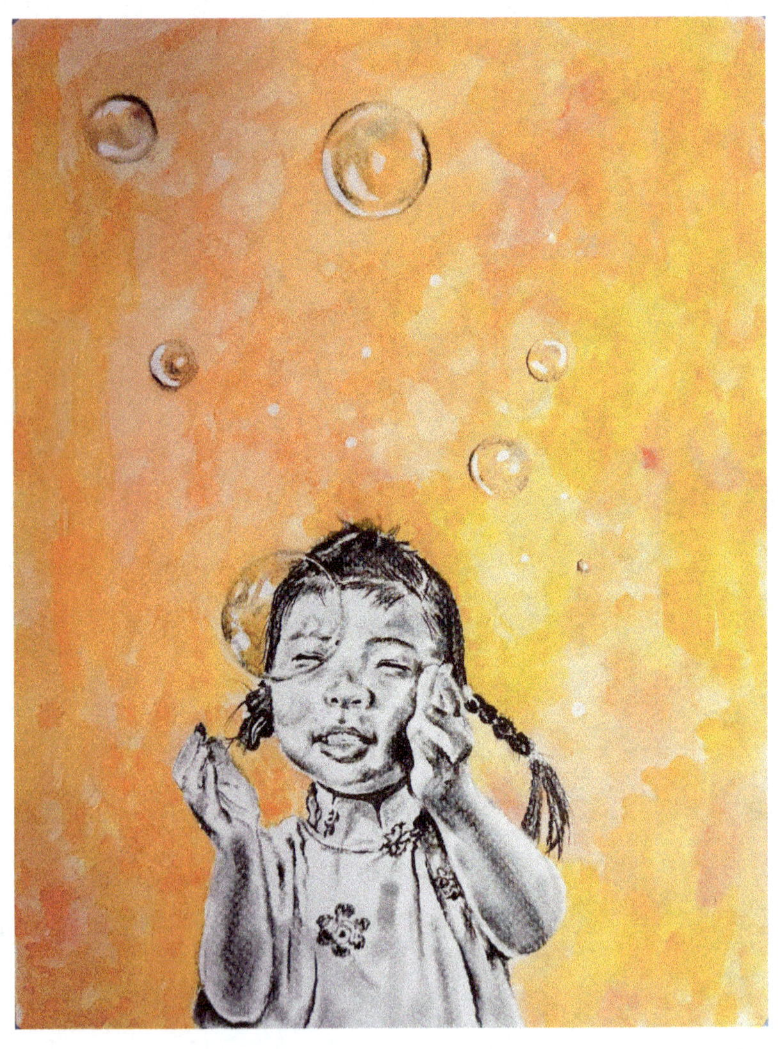

Tickled And Surprised

May you be tickled and surprised by the
beauty He places all around you.

May you sparkle His light to all you meet.

May you feel the tenderness of His kiss on
your wounds.

May you know whatever you face you face
with your tiny hand in His.

May you be snuggled up in His love.

May you always run Home.
For there you are welcome with open arms
Just as you are.

Amen

- Do you feel more like an adult, teenager or child with God? Why do you think that is?

- How might He be tickling and surprising you in your life these days?

- How does He want to tend to your wounds?

- What does it feel like in your heart and body to know God welcomes you with open arms?

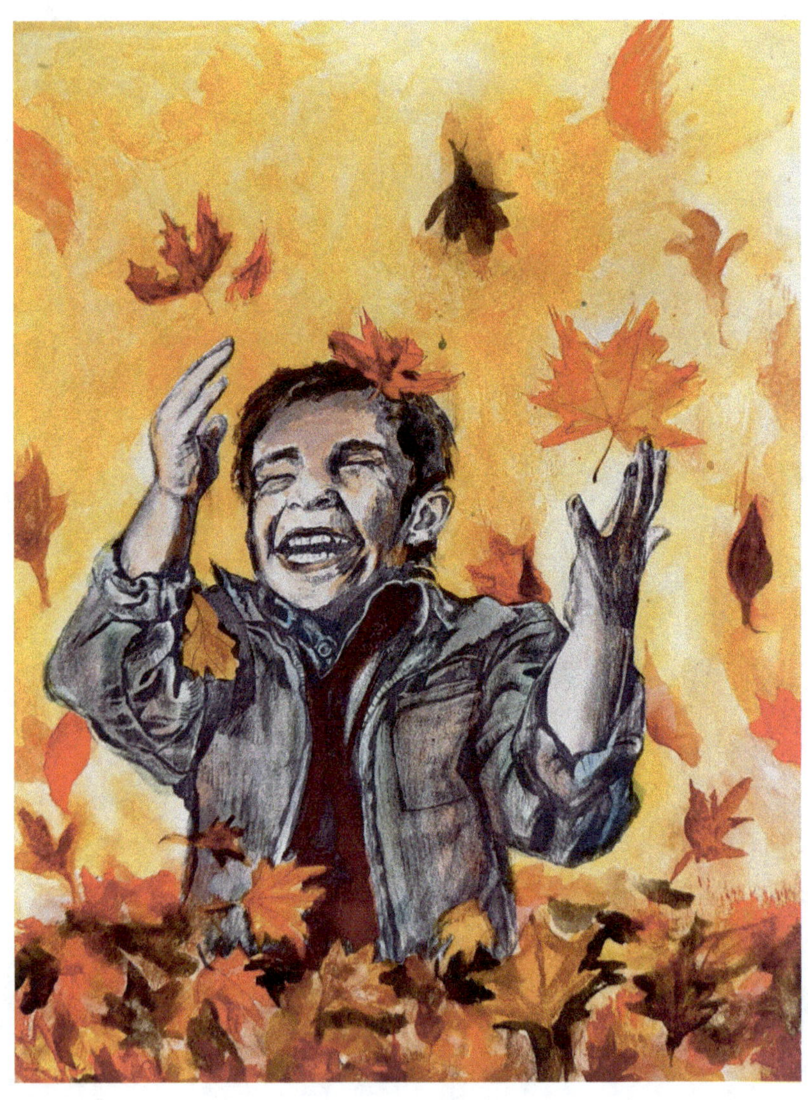

Fall Blessing

Help us to remember the sweetness of the fall.

As the leaves change, remind us that we are changing and lovely too.

Show us what to let go of and what to keep.

Where we are lost, help us to find our way back to You.

Open our eyes to discover the life You have planted within us.

Let the crispness of the air remind us of Your presence and the harvest to come.

And may we rest knowing we are loved.

Amen.

How do you find yourself changing?

Pray and ask God to show you what you need to let go of and what to keep.

What has He planted within you?

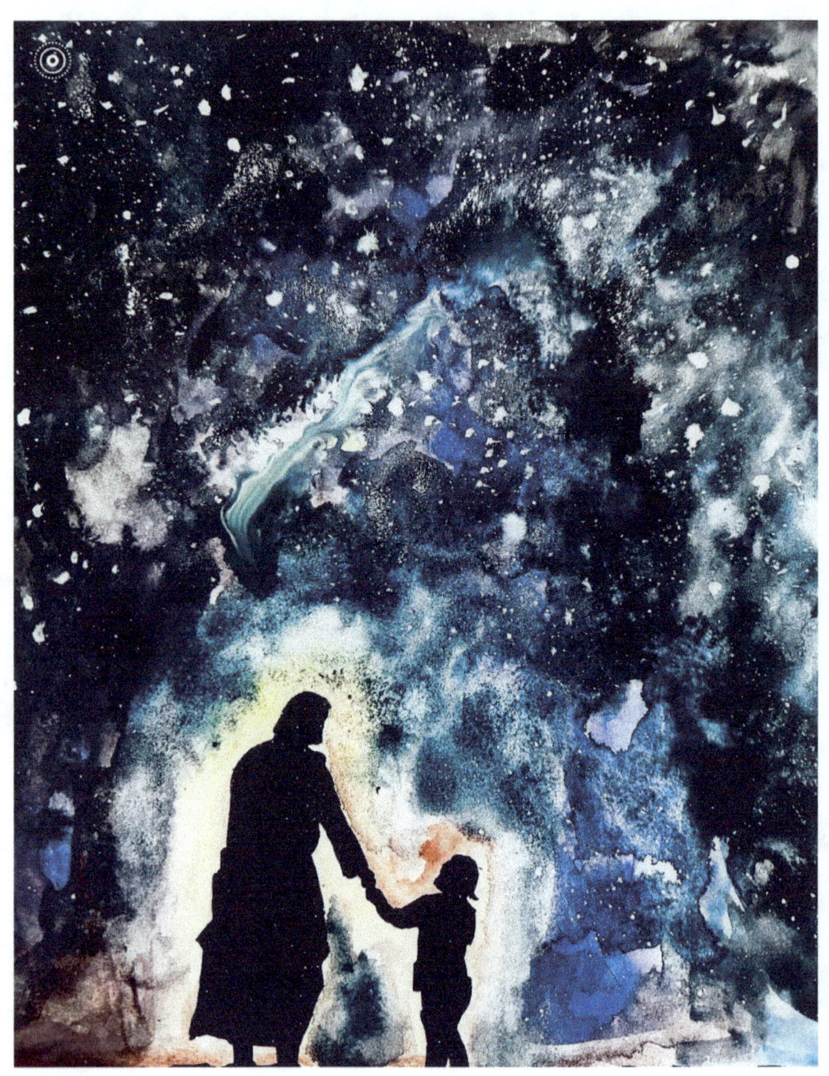

May you **be undone** by this great love today.
May you **be frazzled** by this kindness.
May you **be surprised** by this grace.
May you **be swept away** with His understanding of you.
May you **be flustered** by the gifts of art, beauty and creation.
May you **receive** this love in all the capacity that you can hold.
May you **grow** capacity for more.
May you be **undone** today by Jesus.

May you be **undone** when a hand is extended instead of a harsh punishment.
May you be **undone** by a God who walks with you and even chooses your slow pace.
May you be **undone** by the trust offered. Real trust and goodness.
May you be **undone** by every bird that sings
By every flower that blooms
By every sunbeam and raindrop
May you be **undone** by the rest you are offered when you expect work.
May you be **undone** by this kind of love.
May you be **undone** being loved in all of your flaws and nakedness.
May you be so **undone** that you feel you might break if any more is added to you.
And may Jesus increase your capacity to hold even more.
May you be **undone** by this kind of love.
Be **undone**.

Create a list of times in your life that you felt “Undone” by God?

Include how you felt, and using all your senses to remember what those times were like.

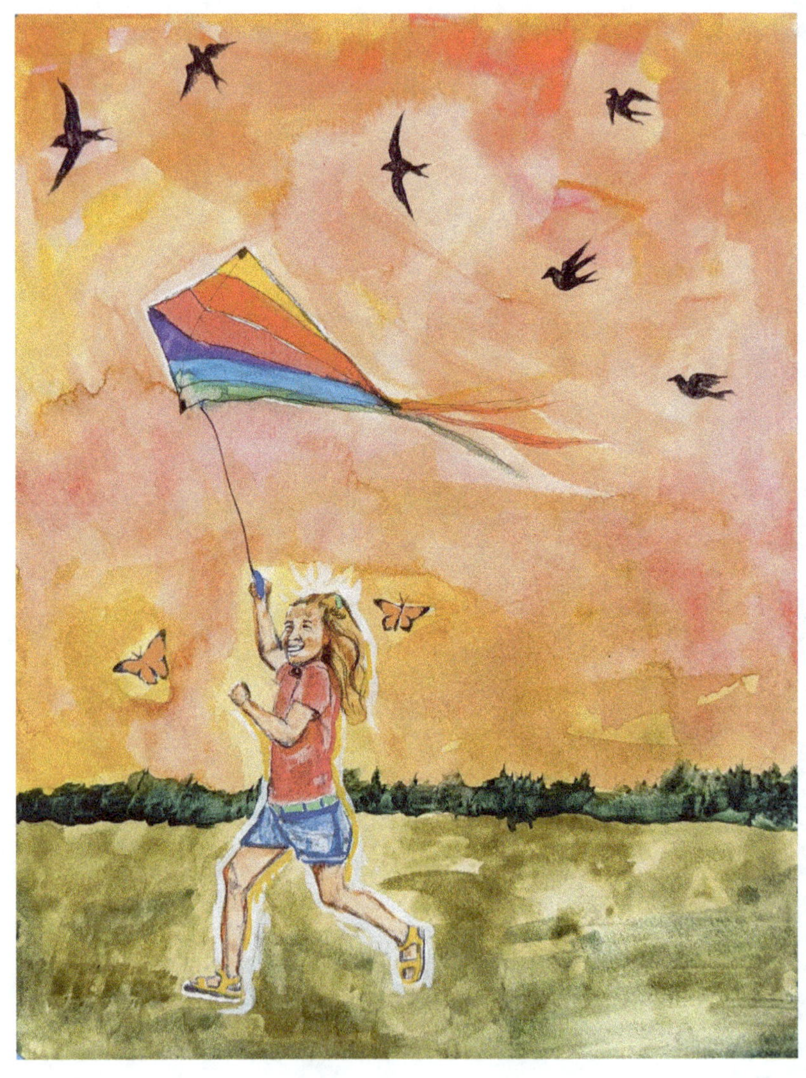

Play

Show me how to play again.

To recklessly put my hand and heart in Yours knowing I am safe and sound. Free me to let go of all the heavy responsibilities and dress clothes. Clothe me in play clothes made to get dirty and tattered.

Show me again how to skip and twirl.

To blow on dandelions and collect rocks.

To swing and climb trees.

To pick wild flowers and hand them with pride as if they were roses on Valentine's Day.

Restore my little self to laugh, to remember that surprises can be good.

Let's catch the wind and swing together. Let's spend hours watching the birds.

We can paint masterpieces with broken crayons. And hide treasures and ring doorbells and run.

We can take two cookies instead of one knowing it's not too much.

Sing songs off key with me. Dance with me.

Let's laugh until we cry together.

And stay up all hours of the night telling secrets and grand stories.

Restore the care free part of me that knows You have me. So I can run amuck with you into kingdoms bigger than I can dream.

Play with me.

What ways do you play with God?

What things did you love to play as a child?

What did you look like? What was the environment around you that made it feel like play?

What keeps you from playing now? What rules do you have around play?

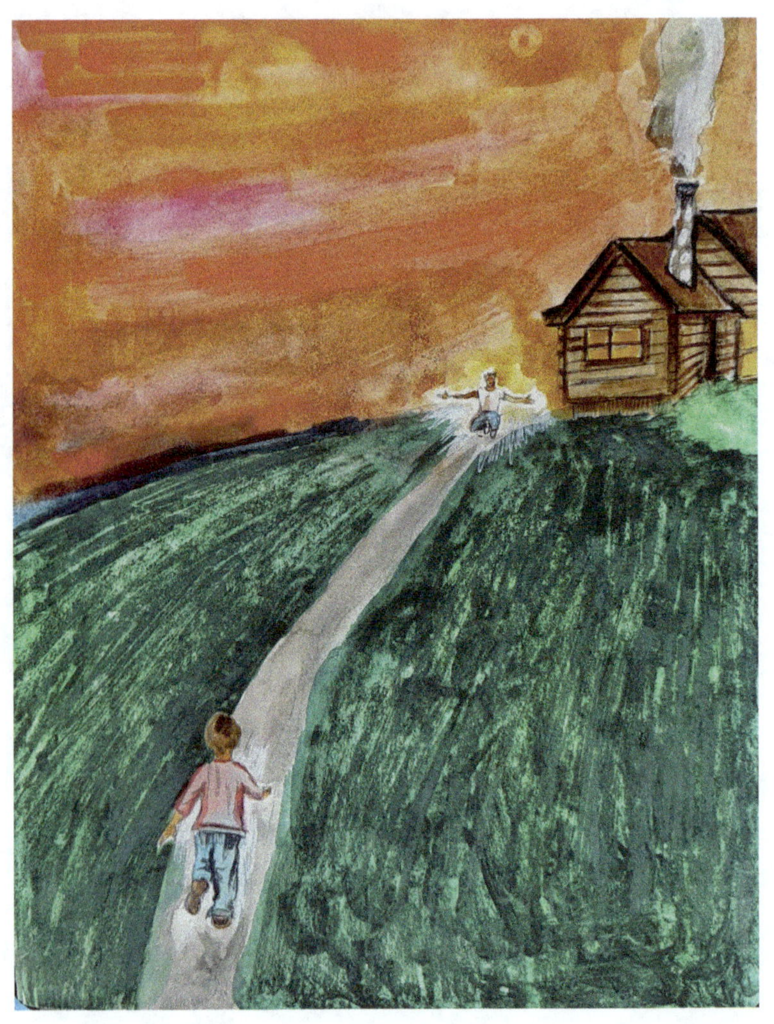

Come Home

When you open your eyes and see beauty-Come back to Me.

When fear overwhelms you-Come back to Me.

When your funny bone is tickled-Come back to Me.

When you experience heartache-Come back to Me.

When things get loud-Come back to Me.

When loneliness wants to overtake you-Come back to Me.

When you are in the mundane day to day-Come back to Me.

When you did that hard thing and you were really brave- Come back to Me.

My door is always open.
My light is always on.
My arms are always wide open.
Come back to me.

In what circumstances and times do you find yourself drifting from God?

What areas are you eager to run home to Him in?

How does it feel in your body to know that the door is always open to you?

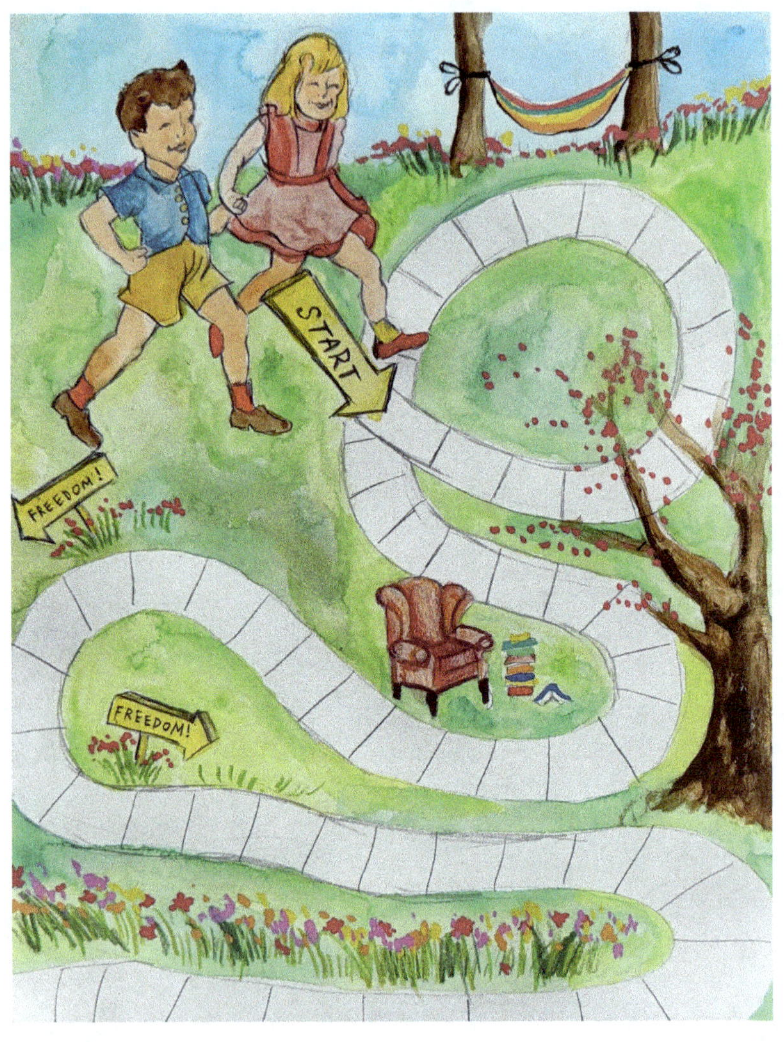
START
FREEDOM!
FREEDOM!

Blessing for a New Start

As we begin again with fresh crisp open pages,
write the new chapter with us.

Let us see life through Your eyes.

May we see ourselves through Your kind eyes.

Help us to let go of any bitterness and resentments,

So we can skip again in freedom and peace.

Give us compassion for ourselves and others.

Show us how to live our lives with deep value and worth, with promise and possibility.

Give us holy courage to face the truth.

And make us brave enough to grieve what is lost and to celebrate what is found.

And please, please God show us all the good rest stops along the way.

What is starting over like for you?

What are the fresh starts that God is inviting you to?

How do you feel?

What can make it easier or harder to start over?

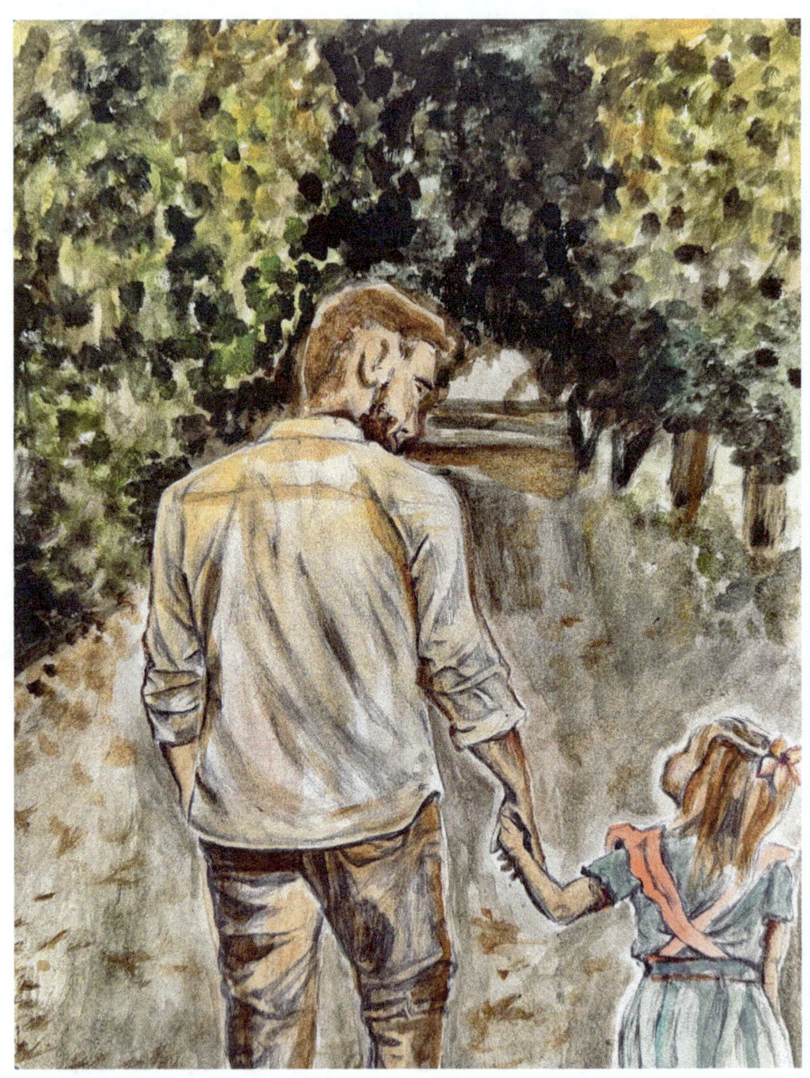

Go with Me

Go with me on unworn paths.

Go with me to places I've long buried.

Go with me into the mystery and uncertainty.

In the pain and broken places.
In my wounds and walk with my limp.

Go with me into the shadows and fears.
Show me the places of surprise and beauty.

Of grace and wonder.

Take me on adventures paved with Your love.

Reveal the real me and the real You.

You go with me. I'll go with You.

Amen

WHERE ARE YOU IN YOUR LIFE RIGHT NOW?

WHAT ARE PLACES THAT YOU TRY TO GO TO ALONE?

WHAT WOULD IT BE LIKE FOR YOU TO INVITE GOD INTO THESE PLACES?

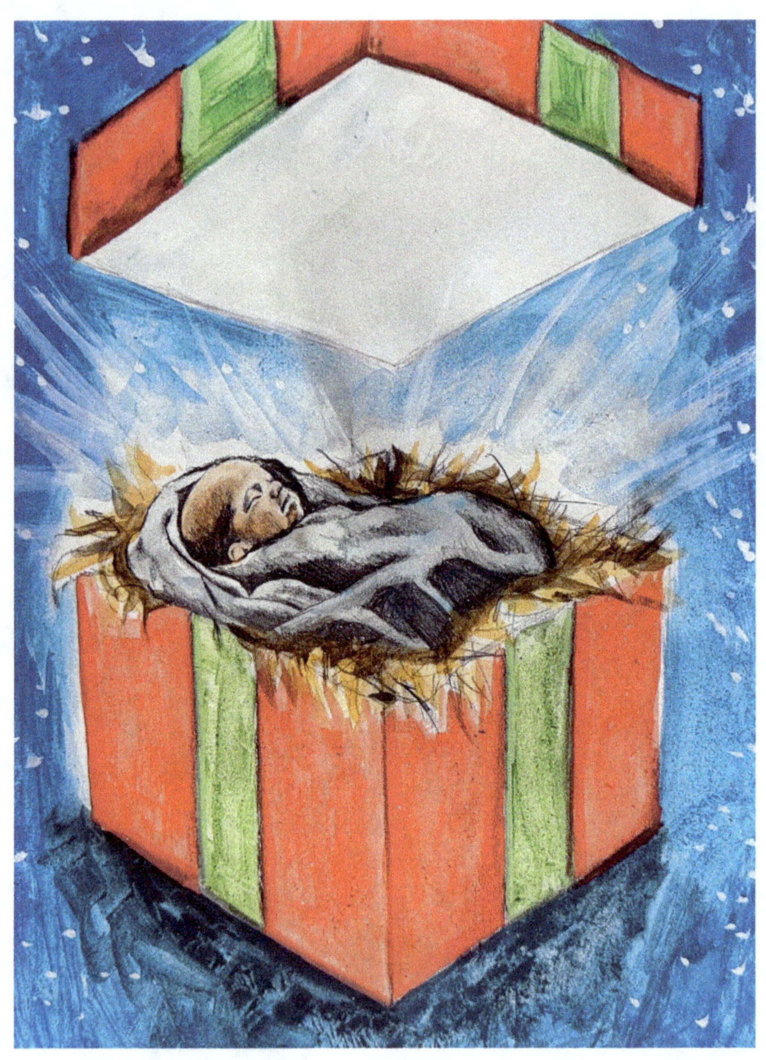

The Gift

In the chaos of the crowded mall
In the screaming of the loneliness
In the rush and hurry as the advent calendar days are counted
Be my intermission in the show.

Slow me down to sense Your presence.
In the glimmer of the Christmas lights,
In the crackle and pop of the fire,
In the twinkle of the star,
The rustling leaves from a mysterious creature in the woods and in the cold air of each of my deep breaths.

Slow me down enough that I might have time to fully receive my gift.

To ferociously and recklessly rip open the paper.

To find The Baby.
To embrace The Baby.

To kiss His face.

So close that I would smell life, find love and wonder again.

Do you hear what I hear?

What is this Christmas season like for you?

What are you looking forward to? What are you dreading?

What ways can you be mindful to slow down long enough to experience the real gift of Jesus for you?

Lagniappe…

In Louisiana, we use this word to say that we are getting or giving a little something "extra." These last blessings were written specifically to bless people that God put on my heart. These groups have been special to me. I have watched them tirelessly serve others or hold painful circumstances with honesty and grace. I thought I'd give you some lagniappe to you and that you might bless some of these people in your own life.

A Blessing for Counselors

May God hold you as you hold hard and heavy things for others.
May He give you insight and wisdom to see what is broken and in need of care.
May He give you ointment to tend to seeping wounds.
May He remind you to care for yourself with the same compassion that you have for others.
May you recognize when you need to rest before you are exhausted.
May you let go of what is not yours to carry.
And may His love and kindness replenish you again.

Amen

Blessing For Foster Parents

May God continue to open His heart wide to you as you have opened yours for His children.
May He give you grace to meet each moment and may He fill in the gaps.
May you be reminded that He is enough and You are enough.
May you give yourself compassion and accept that it's okay to be human.
May you recognize your need to rest and be filled before burnout.
And may you feel God's love holding you every time you open your door.

Amen

A Blessing for Teachers

For the supplies you bought with your own money because it wasn't in the budget

For the germs, Kleenex and crumbs from lunch you pick up

For the ways you see us with so much untapped potential

For doing it again.. and again until we get it.

For being a parent, a comforter, mediator, safety monitor and singer in any given day.

For working tirelessly with menial pay. You are worth so much more.

For smiling when we give you another gift with some sort of apple on it.

For risking your life for us.

Thank you.

May God remind you that what you do truly matters.

May you see and share moments of glory with past students that never will forget you.

May God give you a sense of humor and stamina the week before Christmas Break and a sense of pride when the last day of school arrives. And may you receive your own gold stars and ribbons from God for all that you do for each of us that walk through your door.

May summer super charge you and may you have your own recess. May you be seen and cared for the way you cared for us.

Amen

A Blessing for Widows

May God meet you in the loneliness.
May He ache with you.
May He collect your tears and hold them tightly to his chest.
May He remind you of the good memories.
May He relieve you of any should haves or regret.
May you tangibly feel His presence.
May He provide beauty for you in the midst of the grief.
May God prompt others to come along side of you.
May He fill the gaps with you.
May He lead you in this new, hard unchartered land and show you lovely places in yourself that you never knew.
And may He one day restore your smile again.

Amen

Blessing for First Responders

May God bless you for the times you ran in to danger rather than from it.

For the things you have seen that you cannot unsee.

For the gift of strength you brought showing up to rescue me, attend to my injuries and lead me to safety.

For the courage and bravery to face the unknown, terrifying and catastrophic.

May God hold you holding us.

May He give you a safe place to let go of all you carry for us.

For the physical toll, the night shift, sleep deprived days and for the family you had to leave behind to tend to a stranger.

May God soothe you and lead you to know when you need to be rescued too,

May He restore you for the next call.

Amen

A Blessing for Pastors

May God hold your heart the way you hold others.

May you be free of the unrealistic expectations that we put on you.

May you be reminded that you cannot be everything to everyone.

And when the pressure is intense, may He show you paths of quiet rest and may you trust Him enough to take them. May you serve out of deep rest as much as great need.

May you be brave enough to be honest and ask for help when you need it. And in doing so lead others to accept help too.

May God give you the stamina and strength to love your family and your church well.

May He protect you from the attacks, the temptations, the heavy loads you carry and the weariness.

May you lead out of dependence. May you play with God. May you delight in God and let Him love and delight in you. May He refresh you.

May He refill your heart with hope.

Amen

A Blessing for Caregivers

For the times you couldn't go because you stayed with me, the cancelled plans, the boring long days,

For the dignity and care you gave me when I was the most vulnerable and unlovable,

For the sleepless nights you endured, the worry you carried, the errands you ran to get me all that I needed,

For the strength I borrowed when I was so frail.

Thank you.

For the hyper-vigilance, the advocating phone calls, the tears you held in to be strong for me

Thank you.

For the messes you cleaned up, for the shame you covered and for your presence.

Thank you.

You let God borrow your hands and you loved me well. And there is no way to repay your kindness, faithfulness and love.

May God bless you and may you know that it mattered. May you be seen for all of the invisible ways you have served me. May God fill your cup with strength, goodness and supernatural rest.

Amen

(*For my son Grayson in 2022*)

Write your own Blessings

Fun Prompts to Write a Blessing for others:

1. Ask God to show you someone or some group that you see in life.
2. What do you appreciate and notice about them?
3. What things do you notice that they have to deal uniquely with?
4. What do you wish for them?
5. What do you think God thinks and feels about them?
6. Share what your wrote with a person you want to bless. You can write a card, draw a picture, stick it on a sticky note even mail it to them. Read them to a group. Remember you are reminding others that they are seen, known and appreciated.

Prompts to Write Blessings for yourself:

1. Ask God to show you what He sees and treasures about you?
2. What do you long for or desire?
3. What areas do you need His support and help in?
4. Sincerely write your heart out and give it back to Him.
5. Every so often re-read them. And ask Him to help you see where He was listening and honoring your heart.

About the Author

Kym Byrd is a trained Spiritual Director and facilitator. She currently runs a non-profit ministry called The Byrdhouse Ministries in Milton Georgia. She is passionate about people having deep rest with God, hospitality and caring for those hurting around her. She believes in using every day seemingly small things to point people to a greater understanding of themselves and God. Kym is half Chinese, has been married to Paul for 31 years and is a mom to two grown sons, Grayson and Colby, 8 chickens and one cat. When not at Byrdhouse Ministries, Kym can be seen meeting with friends, watching a film, crafting, beating Paul at Mahjong and traveling. She will also never refuse a good chocolate donut with sprinkles.

To learn more about Kym go to
www.thebyrdhouseministries.com

About the Illustrator

Naya Green is a 17 year old high school student. She is extremely passionate about life and the limitlessness of the imagination. She writes poetry, sculpts with clay and has religiously kept a journal for 4 years now. Her art is a prayer for God, and the way that she connects most deeply with Him. Her most important pastime is to think. She thinks up new ideas and swivels down into new imaginative tunnels. In the fall she will be studying art at Covenant College and then stumbling down whatever path God has for her next!

To learn more about Naya go to
www.nayagreenart.com

www.ingramcontent.com/pod-product-compliance
Lightning Source LLC
LaVergne TN
LVHW010615110826
845149LV00003B/924